# Weather

# KINGFISHER

Kingfisher Publications Plc
New Penderel House
283–288 High Holborn
London WC1V 7HZ
www.kingfisherpub.com

First published by Kingfisher Publications Plc 2006

2 4 6 8 10 9 7 5 3 1

1TR/0606/PRSP/RNB/140MA/F

ISBN-13: 978 0 7534 1309 8
ISBN-10: 0 7534 1309 4


**Senior editor:** Vicky Bywater
**Designer:** Joanne Brown
**Cover designer:** Poppy Jenkins
**Picture research manager:** Cee Weston-Baker
**DTP manager:** Nicky Studdart
**Senior production controller:** Jessamy Oldfield
**Editor and indexer:** Hannah Wilson


Printed in China

Acknowledgements
The publishers would like to thank the following for permission to reproduce their material. Every care has been
taken to trace copyright holders. However, if there have been unintentional omissions or failure to trace copyright
holders, we apologize and will, if informed, endeavour to make corrections in any future edition.
*b* = bottom, *c* = centre, *l* = left, *t* = top, *r* = right

Phototgraphs: *cover* Taxi Getty; 1 Imagebank Getty; 2–3 A&J Verkalk Corbis; 4–5 Photonica Getty; 6*tr* Travelshots Alamy;
6*bl* Reportage Getty; 7 Don Mason Corbis; 8 Stone Getty; 9*tl* Nevada Weir Corbis; 9*r* Photolibrary.com; 10–11 Richard Cooke
Alamy; 11*tl* Simon Fraser Science Photo Library; 12–13 Taxi Getty; 12*cr* Imagebank Getty; 12*bl* Photographer's Choice Getty;
14–15 Still Pictures; 15*tl* Still Pictures; 15*cr* Mike Greenslade Alamy; 16–17 Roy Morsch Zefa Corbis; 16 Photolibrary.com;
18–19 Taxi Getty; 18*b* Remi Benali Corbis; 19*tr* Photolibrary.com; 20–21 Photographer's Choice Getty; 21 Stockbyte Platinum
Getty; 22 National Geographic Society Getty; 23 Still Pictures; 23*tr* Pekka Parviainen Science Photo Library;
24–25 Photolibrary.com; 25*tl* Stone Getty; 25*br* Still Pictures; 26 Stone + Getty; 27*tl* Jim Reed Corbis; 27 Rick Wilking Reuters
Corbis; 28–29 Still Pictures; 29*tl* Still Pictures; 29*br* Iconica Getty; 30–31 Photographer's Choice Getty;
30*l* Photolibrary.com; 31 Iconica Getty; 32–33 Still Pictures; 33*t* Stone Getty; 33*b* Stone Getty; 34–35 Stone Getty;
35 Steve Bloom Alamy; 36–37 National Geographic Society Getty; 36*cr* Jim Reed Corbis; 36*bl* Masterfile; 38–39 Reportage
Getty; 38*bl* Getty Editorial; 39*br* Corbis; 40 Keren Su Corbis; 41*tl* Still Pictures; 41*br* Zute Lightfoot Alamy; 48 Taxi Getty

Commissioned photography on pages 42–47 by Andy Crawford
Project-maker and photoshoot co-ordinator: Jo Connor
Thank you to models Dilvinder Dilan Bhamra, Cherelle Clarke, Madeleine Roffey and William Sartin

KFYK **Kingfisher Young Knowledge**

# Weather

## Caroline Harris

# Contents

# What is weather?

Weather is all the changes that happen in the air. Water, air and heat from the sun work together to make weather.

### Warm and sunny

When the sun is high in the sky and there are not many clouds, the weather is hot and dry. If it is cloudy, the temperature will be lower.

### Let the rain fall

Without water, there would be no life on the earth. Rain helps plants grow and gives animals water to drink.

*temperature – how hot or cold it is*

# Icy water

Water freezes when it is very cold. This changes the weather. Snow falls instead of rain, and water on the ground turns to ice.

**freezes** – *turns to ice*

# Our star

The sun is a burning hot star. It is so bright, it lights up the earth. The sun also helps to make our weather. It heats the land and air to make winds blow, and it warms oceans to make clouds and rain.

## Night and day

The earth spins around once every 24 hours. When one side of the earth faces the sun, it is daytime there. On the other side of earth, it is night-time.

*spins – goes round*

## Sun worship

The Incas lived many years ago in South America. They worshipped the sun. In those days, a lot of people thought the sun was a god because it was so powerful.

## Burning heat

The sun's rays can easily burn people's skin. Stay safe in the sun by covering up and using suncream. Never look straight at the sun.

**worship** – *praying to as a god*

# 10 Blanket of air

The atmosphere is a layer of air that covers the earth. It is where all weather happens. The atmosphere keeps our planet warm and protects it from danger, such as being hit by space rocks.

### Blue skies

The sky looks blue on a clear day. This is because of the way sunlight shines through the earth's atmosphere.

*protects – keeps safe from*

## Breathe in

The atmosphere is made up of a mixture of gases. Both plants and animals need these gases to live.

## Up and away

The atmosphere has five layers. The one closest to earth is the troposphere. This is where clouds form. The layer furthest from earth is the exosphere.

10,000km

EXOSPHERE

satellite

700km

space shuttle

THERMOSPHERE

80km

shooting stars

MESOSPHERE

weather balloon

50km

STRATOSPHERE

12km

TROPOSPHERE

0km
(distance from earth)

*gases* – *shapeless substances, such as air, that are not solid or liquid*

# Changing seasons

Most countries have four seasons: spring, summer, autumn and winter. Seasons change because of the way earth orbits the sun. Each orbit takes a year.

## Earth on the move

The earth tilts, so each pole is nearer the sun and is warmer at different times of the year. When it is summer in the north, it is winter in the south.

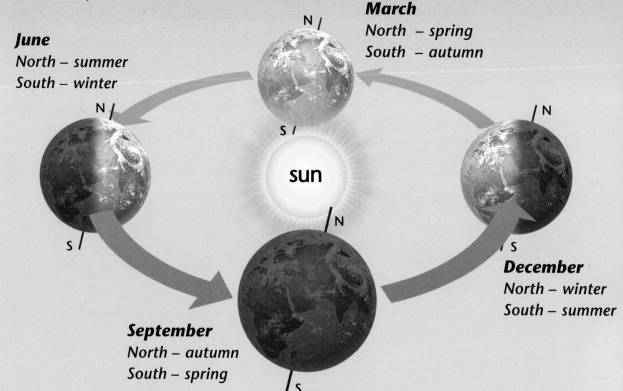

*March*
North – spring
South – autumn

*June*
North – summer
South – winter

sun

*December*
North – winter
South – summer

*September*
North – autumn
South – spring

**orbits** – *moves around*

## Spring and summer

In spring, flowers come out and many animals have babies. The warm weather of summer follows spring.

*spring*

## Autumn and winter

At the end of summer, autumn arrives and the leaves fall off the trees. Then comes chilly winter.

*autumn*

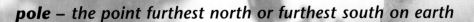

**pole** – *the point furthest north or furthest south on earth*

# World climates

The normal weather in a place is called its climate. There are different types of climate around the world. Some are hot and dry, while others are freezing cold, or warm and wet.

## Icy cold

Antarctica has the coldest climate on earth. The emperor penguins that live there have blubber and special feathers to help them stay warm.

**blubber** – *a layer of fat*

## Hot and dry

Deserts form where the climate is very dry and usually cloudless. They can change from sizzling hot during the day to freezing cold at night.

## Warmed by the ocean

In Cornwall, UK, there are palm trees, which usually grow only in hotter places. A warm sea current makes the climate mild.

*current – a river of warmer or cooler water in the ocean*

# Blowing about

The air in the atmosphere is always on the move, blowing from one place to another. This is wind. Some winds are only gentle breezes. Gales are strong winds that blow tiles off roofs and people off their feet!

**Weather vane**
Whenever the wind blows a weather vane around, the arrow on it turns. The arrow stops once it points the way the wind is blowing.

*breezes – gentle, light winds*

## Flying kites

People have been flying
kites for thousands of years.
The wind lifts the kite, and
the owner can pull or steer
it with a long string.

*steer* – *move something one way or another*

# Wild winds

Strong winds can be very dangerous. They knock down buildings and injure people. But they are also useful – wind turbines can make electricity.

### Dust storm

In places where the soil is dry, strong winds can make huge clouds of dust. These dust storms move quickly and can blow grit into eyes, clothes and hair.

*wind turbines – machines that turn in the wind*

## Twisting winds

A tornado is a spinning funnel of wind that comes from a storm cloud. Some tornadoes are so powerful they can suck a house off the ground.

## Whistling wind

The wind whistles when it blows hard through a small gap. It is the same as when someone whistles through their lips.

*funnel – a tube shape with a wider top and narrower bottom*

# Blue planet

Water covers much of the earth. As the sun warms seas and lakes, it turns the water into vapour. This is in the air, but it cannot be seen.

## The water cycle

Water is always moving. When it rains, water runs into rivers, which flow into the sea. From there, it turns into vapour and makes clouds. Then it rains again.

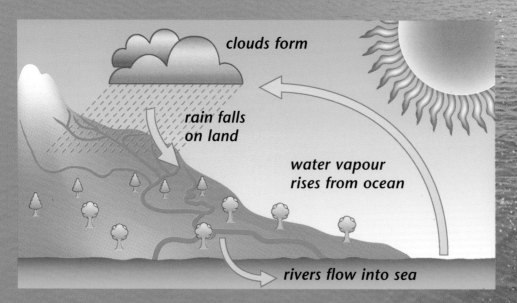

clouds form

rain falls on land

water vapour rises from ocean

rivers flow into sea

**vapour** – *water, mist or fog in the atmosphere*

## Healthy water

Humans are also part of the water cycle. Mineral and tap water were once rain. People need to drink several glasses of water every day to stay healthy.

*dolphins in the ocean*

## Enormous oceans

Oceans cover 72 per cent of the earth's surface. They have a huge effect on our weather. Ocean currents carry with them warm, cold or wet weather.

*cycle – events that happen again and again*

# Mist and clouds

Clouds can be made from tiny drops of water or from ice crystals. They are formed when warm air holding water vapour cools down. Clouds come in all shapes and sizes.

## Fluffy cumulus

A cloud's name describes how high up it is and what it looks like. For example, the fluffy clouds seen in warm weather are called cumulus.

*crystals – tiny bits of ice*

## Glowing in the night

Some clouds glow in the dark, just after sunset. They look bright blue and are criss-crossed with wavy lines.

## Tiger in the mist

Mist and fog are cloud near the ground. They usually form in cool weather. This tiger's home in the jungle is very wet, so it is misty there even though it is warm.

*jungle – a hot, wet place full of trees and plants*

# Out in the rain

A raindrop is made when tiny drops of water in a cloud touch and join together. The raindrop gets larger and heavier, and finally it falls to the ground as rain.

## The shape of rain

Rain may look like lines, but each raindrop is usually the shape of a sphere. Most are small – the size of a pencil tip.

*sphere – a ball shape*

## Carried by the wind

Storms produce enormous, heavy raindrops. Strong winds keep the rain up in the air for a long time, so the drops get really big.

## Leafy umbrella

Like humans, many animals like to shelter from the rain. Orang-utans hold handfuls of leaves above their heads to stop getting wet.

*produce – make*

# Stormy days

A thunderstorm happens when clouds grow bigger and taller, and gather more and more energy. Every day, there can be as many as 40,000 storms crashing down around the world.

## Lightning strikes

Lightning is a spark of electricity that makes the air glow. It can move between clouds or shoot down to the ground, onto trees or buildings.

*energy* – *power, force*

## High as a mountain

Thunderclouds can be enormous. In very severe storms, they can be taller than a mountain!

## Hurricane damage

A hurricane is a group of thunderstorms that spin. At the centre is a calm circle called the eye. When a hurricane hits the land, it can cause a lot of damage.

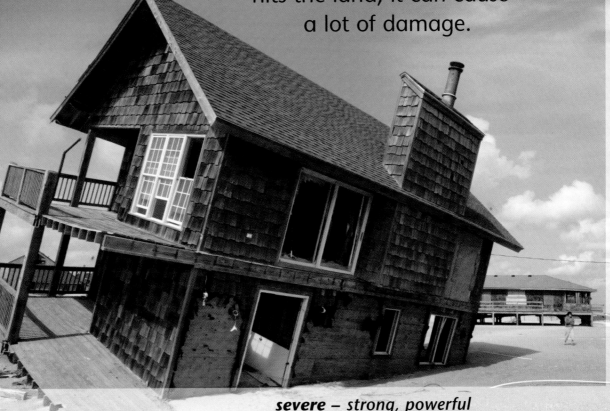

*severe – strong, powerful*

# Wet and dry

Some parts of the world are rainy and wet. Other places are very dry. In deserts, years may pass without rain. But in the jungle, it can rain heavily all year long.

**Pumping water**
During a drought, there is not much rain. In very dry areas, people may have to walk to a well to get drinking water.

**drought** – *when the weather is drier than normal*

## Water everywhere

When a lot of rain falls, it can cause floods. These are lakes of water that can cover a large area, even a whole city.

## Dry earth

When it does not rain for a long time, the earth can become so dry and hard that it cracks.

**well** – *a deep hole that leads to water under the ground*

# Big freeze

When water gets very cold, it freezes into solid, slippery ice. You can see this as frost on plants and lawns, or the frozen, hard layer on a pond.

### Handful of ice

Hailstones are balls of ice made in the thunderclouds. They fall like rain and the largest ones can be the size of a grapefruit. Ouch!

**solid** – hard, not liquid

## Feathery crystals

Frost forms when air near the ground is wet and so cold that it freezes. When it is warmer, this wetness makes dew instead.

## Mountains of ice

Ice weighs less than water. This is why huge icebergs float. But only a small part of the ice can be seen. The rest is hidden underwater.

*dew – drops of water on, for example, grass, especially in the morning*

# Flakes of snow

Snowflakes are made from ice that forms high up in the clouds. In warm weather, the ice melts and falls to the ground as rain or sleet. If it is cold enough, it falls as snow.

## Snowfall

Snowflakes are snow crystals that are stuck together. Big flakes form when it is just below freezing. This is when the crystals are stickiest.

*sleet – rain mixed with snow or hail*

## Cosy snow

Snow can keep you warm! The Inuit people, who live in the Arctic, make buildings called igloos from blocks of snow.

## Snow shapes

Most snow crystals have six sides, but they never look exactly the same as each other. They all form different, beautiful patterns.

*Arctic – the area around the North Pole*

Light **shows**

Sometimes, water and ice crystals can make light look very colourful or unusual. They can cause amazing effects, such as sun dogs and the beautiful glowing light of a rainbow.

### Colourful rainbow

When it rains and is sunny at the same time, it is sometimes possible to see a rainbow. This is especially clear if a dark cloud lies behind the rain.

*effects – results*

## Sun dogs

The two lights either side of the sun are called sun dogs. They happen when sunlight shines through ice crystals in a particular way. They can have tails of light and look like dogs.

*particular* – *special*

# Extreme weather

Sometimes the weather can be wild and dangerous. Hurricanes, floods, wildfires and droughts are all types of extreme weather.

### Water power

Floods may stretch over huge distances and cause a lot of damage. They can leave people stranded, so that they need to be rescued by helicopter or boat.

### Fighting fire

Wildfires break out in hot weather. This is because trees and plants dry out, and then burn easily.

*extreme – most unusual or severe*

## El Niño

This is a current of warm
water in the Pacific ocean
that happens every few years.
It can cause terrible floods,
droughts and storms.

**wildfires** – *fires in forests or grassland*

# Rain or shine?

Weather forecasts tell us what the weather will be like for the next few days. Scientists use instruments and computers to make these forecasts.

## Storm spotting

Trucks fitted with radar can find storms that are far away. Scientists then follow the storms and measure their strength.

## Damp seaweed

There are easy ways of forecasting weather. For example, seaweed gets fat and floppy in wet air. This means that rain is coming.

*instruments – tools used to take measurements*

## Weather balloons

Scientists use balloons to lift instruments high into the sky. These then measure the weather.

**radar** – *an instrument that can locate objects far away*

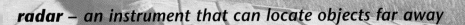

# Future weather

The earth's climate naturally goes through times when it is a lot warmer or icier than it is today. However, many scientists believe that humans are changing the weather.

## Smokey cars

The weather may be changing because of pollution. It traps too much of the sun's heat. This heat would normally escape into space.

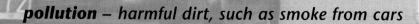

*pollution* – *harmful dirt, such as smoke from cars*

## Getting warmer

Earth's climate is heating up. This makes ice melt and break away from icebergs and glaciers. As a result, the levels of the oceans rise and flood areas of land.

## Help for farmers

Scientists are now better at forecasting weather several months ahead. Farmers use these forecasts to help them decide which crops to plant each year.

*glaciers – solid rivers of ice*

# Riding the wind

## Making a kite

Kites soar in the sky because the wind pushes them upwards. Decorate yours with an animal face – try a tiger!

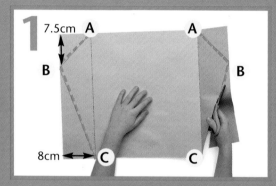

7.5cm  **A**    **A**

**B**    **B**

8cm  **C**    **C**

Following the measurements shown, draw lines between A and C, A and B, and B and C. Cut the paper from C to B and B to A.

## You will need

- Sheet of A3 paper
- Ruler
- Pencil
- Scissors
- Felt-tip pens
- Sticky tape
- Hole punch
- 2 long drinking straws
- Coloured tissue paper
- Thin cotton string
- Thin stick

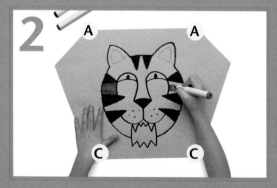

**2**    **A**    **A**

**C**    **C**

Turn the paper over and decorate your kite. You could draw a tiger. Make sure A is at the top of the kite and C is at the bottom.

**3**    **B**    **B**

Put sticky tape on the corners of the paper at B. Then use the hole punch to make holes through the tape 2.5cm from the edge, at B.

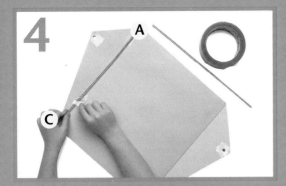

Turn the kite over. Use the sticky tape to fasten the straws on both sides of the paper along the line between A and C.

Using the scissors, cut strips of coloured tissue paper 20cm long. Stick the strips along the bottom edge of the kite.

*Now your kite is ready to fly! Take a trip to the park and ask an adult to throw the kite high into the air. Pull it along, holding tightly onto the stick.*

Thread 80cm of string through the punched-out holes and tie the ends together. The sides of the kite should bend inwards slightly. Wind another, long piece of string onto the stick. Tie the end to the middle of the string on the kite.

# Sun dancer

## Flashing lights

Your sun dancer will sparkle in the sunlight. If you place it near fruit bushes, it can help to scare away birds and stop them eating berries.

**1**

Place two CDs on paper with the shiny side facing down. Spread on glue. Stick the CDs together. Leave to dry. Repeat with the other CDs.

## You will need
- 6 blank CDs
- Glue for plastic/paper
- Shiny cardboard
- Pencil
- Scissors
- Thread (6 x 20cm, 2 x 25cm, 1 x 35cm)
- String (35cm)
- Small bells
- Stick (25cm)

**2**

Draw six moons and six stars on cardboard. Cut them out. Stick two star shapes together, shiny side out. Repeat with all shapes.

**3**

Ask an adult to make a small hole in the point of each star and moon. Poke 20cm of thread into each hole and pull it halfway through.

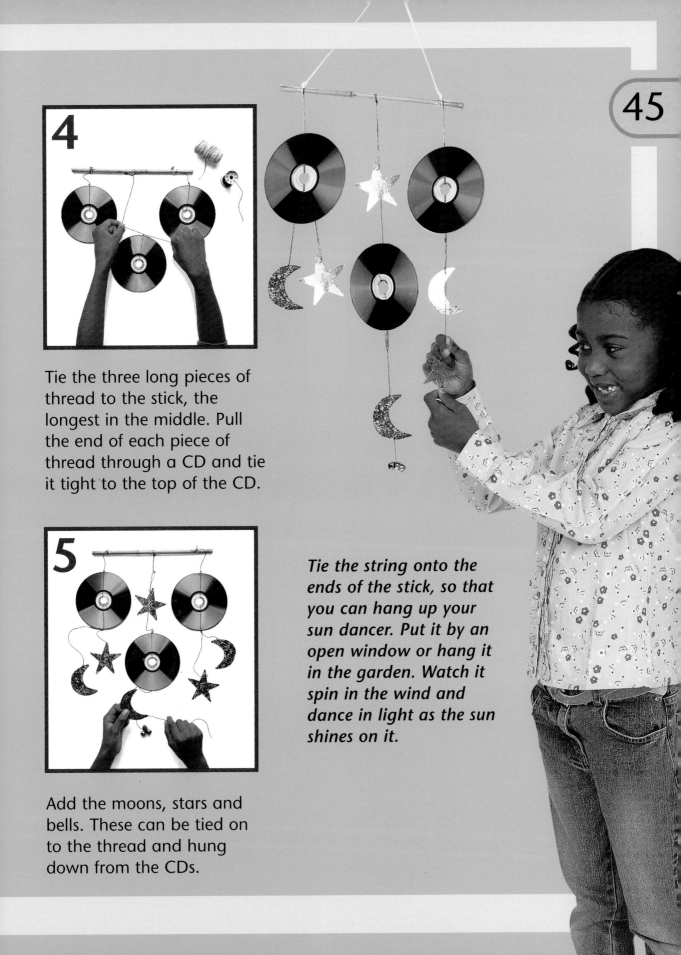

**4**

Tie the three long pieces of thread to the stick, the longest in the middle. Pull the end of each piece of thread through a CD and tie it tight to the top of the CD.

**5**

Add the moons, stars and bells. These can be tied on to the thread and hung down from the CDs.

*Tie the string onto the ends of the stick, so that you can hang up your sun dancer. Put it by an open window or hang it in the garden. Watch it spin in the wind and dance in light as the sun shines on it.*

# Creating colours

## Make a rainbow

See how water is able to split light into different colours to make an amazing rainbow in your home.

### You will need
- Glass jar
- Small mirror
- Torch
- Water jug

**1** Place the glass jar on a table in a room with plain, light walls. Use the jug to half fill the jar with warm water.

**2** Put the mirror in the jar and tilt it slightly upwards. Draw the curtains and turn out the lights so the room is very dark.

*rainbow*

*Shine the torch on to the mirror and a rainbow should appear on the wall.*

# Swirling winds

## Make a tornado

The swirling water in this experiment acts in the same way as the spinning winds of a wild tornado.

### You will need
- Big, plastic bottle with cap
- Washing up liquid
- Food colouring
- Glitter

**1**

Fill the bottle with water and add three drops of washing up liquid and some food colouring. Shake in some glitter, which will act like the dust that a tornado picks up.

*Screw the cap back on tightly then swirl your bottle around in circles. Put it down quickly and watch what happens.*

*tornado*

# Index